My Big Book of EASTER Activities

10 9 8 7 6 5 4 3 2 1

Library of Congress Control Number: 2019948681

Cover design by Louise Millar
Cover artwork by Clare Beaton

Print ISBN: 978-1-63158-456-5
Ebook ISBN: 978-1-63158-458-9

Printed in China

My Big Book of EASTER Activities

Make and color Decorations, creative crafts, and More!

Clare Beaton

FOR YOUNG READERS

Treasure not Rubbish

Here is a selection of things you can keep to use for the projects in this book and for others too.

Lace bits

Look out for little bits of lace, old lacy placemats, and net curtains.

Egg cartons

Egg cartons are very useful. Use them for making projects or even as storage for small treasures like buttons.

Old yarn

Keep ends of balls of yarn. Even small lengths are useful.

Plastic bags

Keep thicker, colored ones. It doesn't matter if there is writing or pictures on them.

candy wrappers

Keep jewel-colored foils and cellophane.

Old shirts and scraps of material

cardboard, cardboard boxes, and tubes

Small, large, thick, thin and corrugated are all useful.

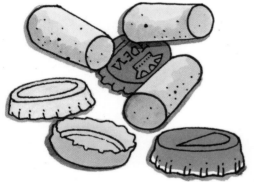

corks and metal tops

Rinse bottle tops and dry them.

Buttons

Every color and size.

Giftwrap, magazines, and catalogues

Save old giftwrap and smooth it flat with a cool iron. Keep old magazines and catalogues.

Large plastic bottles

Wash and remove any labels. See-through and colored bottles are both useful.

Twigs, pinecones, and shells

Whilst on walks in the countryside, park, or on the beach, pick up interesting natural objects.

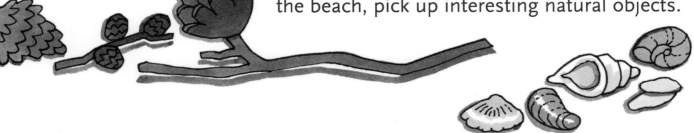

Before you begin

- Always take great care with sharp tools such as scissors, needles, and knives.
- Always cover work surfaces with newspaper before you start to paint or varnish your work.
- When using a craft knife always cut away from hands. Use thick cardboard or something similar under whatever you are cutting. Cut slowly and lightly several times.
- Wash your hands and wear an apron before preparing food.

Some basic tools and materials:
paint and brushes
varnish
glue
scissors
craft knife
paper
card
colored pencils
felt-tip pens

This caterpillar will be crawling through the pages with you. See if you can spot it each time.

Look for flowers to press and use to make the cards on the opposite page. Choose perfect flowers with nice long stems. Only pick one or two wild flowers where several are growing.

Pressed flowers

Flowers can be preserved forever by pressing all the moisture out of them. When picking wild flowers remember to leave plenty for other people to enjoy.

What you will need
★ flowers
★ blotting paper and flower press or heavy books!
★ cardboard or paper
★ glue and brush

1

Make sure your flowers are undamaged. Arrange them on blotting paper. Cover with more paper.

2

Press with flower press or use heavy books as weights. After a few days check to see if the flowers are dry.

3

When completely dry remove carefully. Cut paper or cardboard to make pictures or greeting cards. Arrange flowers and glue into place.

TIP
Cover flowers with sticky-backed plastic to protect them.

Don't be afraid to stick some flowers upside down or sideways.

Bookmarks make great gifts.

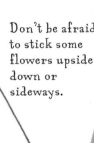

Cut out patterned paper to make vase or pot shapes.

For a calendar, add a loop of ribbon, border, and small calendar. (Get them from newsagents or stationers.)

Painted and stained eggs

Blowing eggs

You can make beautiful Easter egg decorations to hang on a small branch. First you need to prepare the eggs.

What you will need
★ eggs
★ needle
★ small bowl

1

Ask a grown-up to help you make the holes.

Make a small hole with a needle at the narrow end of each egg and a larger hole at the other end.

2

Hold the egg carefully over a bowl and blow through the smaller hole. Use the eggs later for baking or scrambled eggs.

For decorating your eggs

- paints
- felt-tip pens
- brushes
- matchsticks
- thread
- thin ribbons and tassels
- masking tape
- colored foil
- glue
- small pictures

Tie some thread around a matchstick making a long loop. Gently push the matchstick through the larger hole and hang up.

Fabergé eggs

A Russian jeweller called Carl Fabergé made famous Easter eggs out of precious metals and marble. They were decorated with pearls and diamonds and often contained a secret message!

What you will need

★ blown eggs (see page 8)
★ paints and brushes
★ ribbon or braid
★ glue
★ sequins or jewels
★ section of cardboard tube

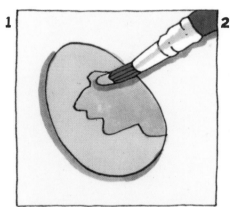

1 Paint each egg in a bright color. Leave to dry.

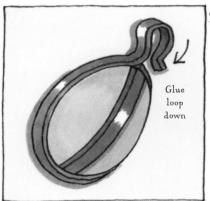

2 Glue ribbon or braid around each egg. Glue on a second piece leaving enough to form a loop at the top of the egg.

Glue loop down

3 Glue sequins and jewels all over the egg between the ribbon. Glue one large jewel at the bottom.

Cut out small pictures to glue on to egg.

Paint and decorate a section of cardboard tube to display eggs.

Glue thin ribbons around egg and a tassel onto the bottom.

You can decorate hard-boiled eggs as well but do not eat them once decorated.

Cut small shapes out of masking tape and stick on egg. Paint over egg and remove tape when dry.

Roll colored foil into balls and squiggles and glue onto painted egg.

Perfect pancakes

Pancakes are delicious with sweet or savory fillings.

What you will need

To make 6 large pancakes

★ 3.5 oz. (100 g) plain flour
★ large pinch of salt
★ 1 egg
★ 8.5 fl. oz. (250 ml) milk
★ butter for frying
★ fillings (see picture 4)

★ sieve
★ mixing bowl
★ measuring jug
★ wooden spoon
★ frying pan

1

Sift the flour and salt into the mixing bowl. Add the egg and half the milk. Mix well to make a smooth batter.

2

Add the rest of the milk and leave the batter to rest for 20 minutes. Meanwhile choose your filling.

3

Put the batter in the jug to make pouring easier.

Cook for 2–3 minutes each side.

With a grown-up helping, heat a pat of butter in the frying pan. When hot pour enough batter to cover base of pan. Turn once.

4

chocolate sauce   grated cheese or ham

jam   sugar and lemon

Add cheese or ham to the pancake when it's still in the frying-pan or a sweet filling when the pancake is on your plate.

Egg one out

Each of these eggs has a pair—except one.
Can you spot the odd one out?

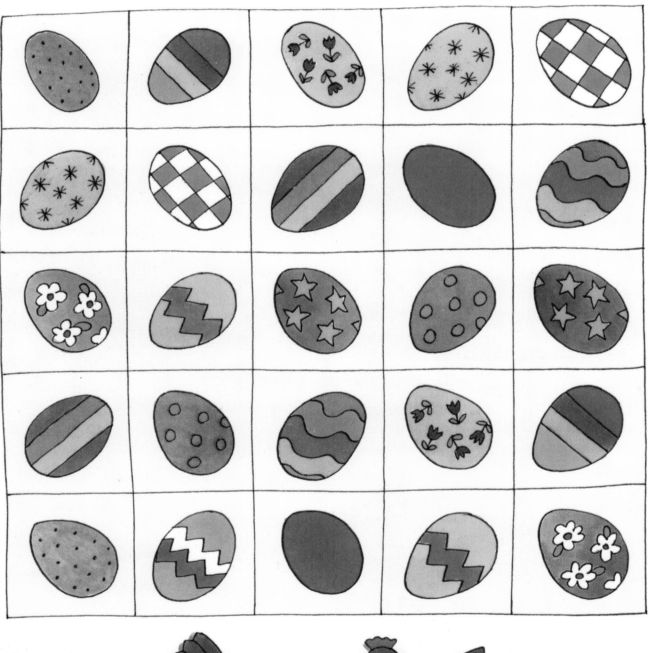

Growing seeds

cress

Growing your own salad cress is easy. It only takes a few days before it is ready to eat.

What you will need
★ packet of cress seeds
★ paper towel
★ plate
★ water

1

Place several layers of paper towel on the plate and sprinkle it with water until damp. Scatter seeds on top. Place on a light windowsill.

2

Keep seeds and paper damp and watch the cress grow. When grown, cut with scissors and eat.

Serving suggestions:
Egg and cress sandwiches.
Mix into salads.

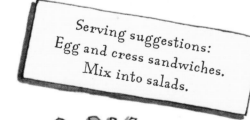

Eggheads
Draw faces on broken eggshells and keep upright with a small piece of clay. Push some crumpled paper towel down inside the shells. Dampen it, sprinkle on some cress seeds, and watch the "hair" sprout.

Bean sprouts

Grow your own bean sprouts in a jam jar. They take about a week to be ready to eat. Keep them in the fridge once they're ready.

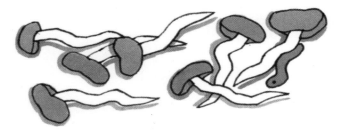

what you will need

★ dried mung beans
★ sieve
★ bowl
★ glass jam jar
★ water
★ piece of net or muslin
★ rubber band or string

1

Wash the beans in the sieve under a cold tap. Leave them in a bowl of water overnight.

2

Put the beans into the jam jar and tie the piece of net or muslin over the top using the rubber band or string. Rinse out beans with water, drain, and place on a sunny windowsill.

3

Continue rinsing and draining the beans until all have sprouted. Rinse and eat.

Serving suggestions:
Add to salads—served with a dressing.
Honey and Lemon Dressing
2 tbsp lemon juice
1 tbsp runny honey
1½ tbsp olive oil
pepper and salt
Put all the ingredients in a screw-top jar. Shake to mix.

Easter cards

Zigzag card

What you will need

★ plain paper and tracing paper
★ pencil, felt-tip pens, or paint and brushes
★ scissors

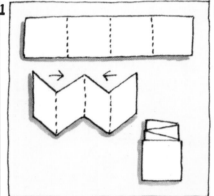

1 Cut paper into a strip 15 in. long and 3.5 in. wide. Fold into four.

2 Draw on a rooster using the template opposite and the instructions on page 55. Cut out.

3 Open out and decorate with felt-tip pens and/or paint.

Eggshell card

What you will need

★ plain paper and tracing paper
★ glue
★ eggshells, broken into small pieces
★ pencil, felt-tip pens, or paint and brushes

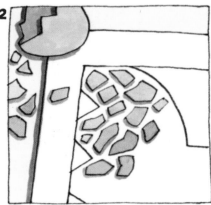

1 Cut card into a piece 8.5 in. x 4 in.

Cut card to size and fold. Draw on a rooster using template opposite.

2 Cover the rooster shape with glue and then eggshells. Leave to dry.

3 Paint or felt-tip around the rooster and decorate the border.

Yarn card

What you will need

★ plain card and tracing paper
★ pencil
★ glue
★ thick colored yarn
★ small black bead

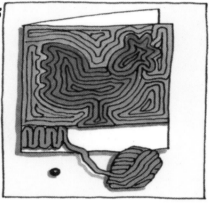

1

Cut card into a piece 8.5 in. x 4 in. and fold. Draw in a rooster using template below. Leave egg out.

2 Push strands close together.

Cover the rooster shape with glue. Starting at the top, carefully cover it with yarn.

3

Glue and cover the rest of card in different colors until finished. Glue bead on for eye.

ROOSTER TEMPLATE

Trace template onto tracing paper.

Turn over and scribble over the shape with a soft pencil.

Turn over and tape into position on paper or card. Draw over lines.

Easter customs and traditions

Easter is the most important Christian holiday. On Easter Sunday Christians celebrate the Resurrection—this was Jesus' return to life three days after he died on the cross.

Passover is a spring festival celebrated by Jews remembering how God rescued the Jews from slavery under the Egyptians.

Long before Christian times people held festivals to mark the end of winter and the beginning of spring. The word Easter probably comes from Eastre—the goddess of spring.

Easter eggs are given and eaten in many countries—they are a symbol of new life. Children in some countries believe that the Easter rabbits bring the eggs. Decorating eggs is a custom followed all over the world.

Egg-rolling is a popular game in England and America. An annual contest takes place on the lawns of the White House in Washington, DC. Try egg-rolling with your friends using hard-boiled, decorated eggs. The first egg to reach the finish is the winner.

Easter has no fixed date. Easter Sunday falls between March 22nd and April 25th. It is the first Sunday after the full moon on or after March 21st.

Egg hunts are fun, too. Hide small candies and chocolate eggs either inside or outside in a garden or park. Collect them in small pots or baskets (see pages 18 and 19).

Easter is a time for feasting and enjoying traditional foods. **Hot Cross Buns** were originally eaten on Good Friday (the day Jesus died) and they have a cross on top.

Simnel cake is a fruit cake with marzipan on top decorated with marzipan balls representing the twelve Apostles.

Lamb symbolizes Jesus (the "Lamb of God") and lamb-shaped cakes are popular in some European countries.

Easter parades provide an opportunity to show off new clothes and fancy Easter bonnets. Thousands join in the parade along 5th Avenue in New York City.

Make an Easter bonnet yourself by decorating a hat with paper streamers, ribbons, flowers, chicks, and rabbit ears.

Easter baskets

You will need a pair of scissors and four brass paper fasteners to assemble these two Easter baskets

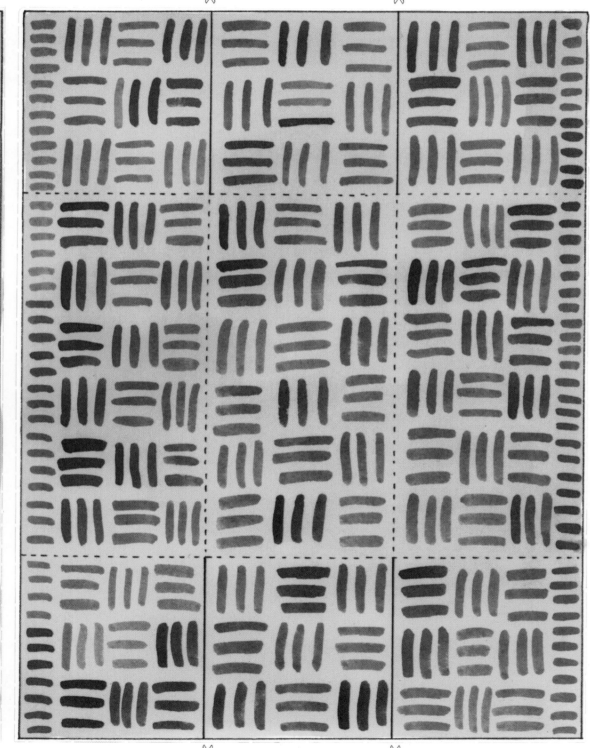

HANDLE FOR EASTER BASKET

1. Copy these patterns onto thin cardboard. Cut along solid lines.

2. Fold along dotted lines outwards from bottom.

3. Turn over. Draw together overlapping sides to form a point.

4. Make a small hole through the three pieces. Push in paper fasteners, handle first.

5. Fold back fastener inside. Repeat on other side.

Easter decorations

Paper flowers

What you will need
- ★ crêpe or tissue paper
- ★ scissors
- ★ thin wire
- ★ green paper
- ★ glue
- ★ twigs

1

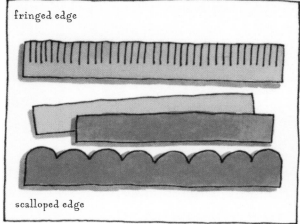

fringed edge

scalloped edge

Cut crêpe or tissue paper into 5 in. x 1.5 in. strips. Cut some long edges into scallops, some into fringes.

2

Open petals out. →

Holding the straight edges of strips roll up and tightly wind 2 in. length of wire around the bottom edge, leaving some free.

3

Cut leaf shapes from green paper and glue to twigs. Wind the wire round the twigs to attach flowers.

20

Hanging eggshells

See if you can collect some eggshells. When painted they make lovely decorations and look very festive when hung from a vase full of dry branches.

What you will need

★ egg shells
★ paint, varnish (if you want), and brushes
★ needle and yarn
★ small branches

1

Paint your half shells with a variety of bright colors and patterns. Leave to dry. Varnish if you want to.

2

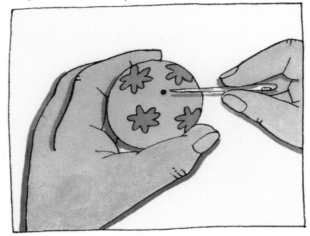

Holding each half shell carefully pierce a hole in the top with your needle. Ask a grown-up to help.

3

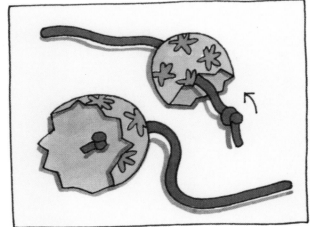

Thread a length of yarn through the hole and knot on the inside of the shell. Tie to a branch.

Nest cakes

To make 6 cakes

- ★ 4 tablespoons golden syrup
- ★ 5 oz. (150 g) margarine or butter
- ★ 2 oz. (50 g) cocoa butter
- ★ 5 oz. (150 g) shredded wheat
- ★ small sweet eggs

- ★ saucepan
- ★ wooden spoon
- ★ greased baking tray
- ★ bowl

1 Put the first three ingredients into a saucepan. Ask a grown-up to stir them over a low heat until melted.

2 Break the shredded wheat into small pieces. Put in the bowl and pour in the melted mixture. Mix well.

3 Place small amounts on a greased baking tray. Mold into nest shapes. Leave to harden.

4 Arrange small sweet eggs inside the nests.

Paper boats

These boats are very simple to make. Build a whole fleet and have races with your friends. You can personalize them with names and colored flags.

What you will need
★ double sheet of broadsheet newspaper, folded
★ felt-tip pens
★ toothpicks
★ colored paper and glue

1

Fold the folded double sheet into two and fold corners down.

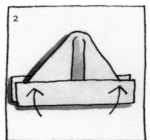

2

Fold up bottom edges.

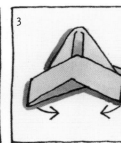

3

Bring ends together.

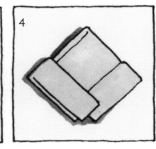

4

Flatten sideways.

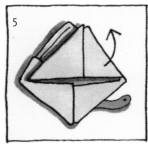

5

Turn top corner up.

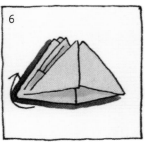

6

Turn back corner up to match.

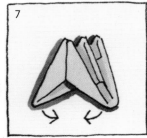

7

Bring ends together.

8

Flatten sideways.

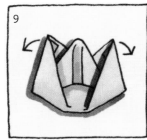

9

Gently open by pulling ends down.

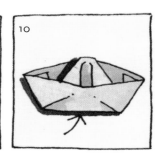

10

Open out central point from bottom.

Glue pieces of colored paper on to toothpicks to make flags.

Decorate your boats using felt-tip pens.

spot the difference

Can you spot ten differences between these two pictures?
Answers on page 95.

Butterfly

What you will need
★ thick colored paper
★ pencil
★ scissors
★ sticky shapes
★ glue
★ sequins
★ scraps of colored paper
★ clothes pins

1

3 in. 4 in.

Fold thick paper in half. Draw and then cut out wing shapes.

2

Decorate both sides with sticky shapes or glue on sequins and cut or torn colored paper shapes.

3

Cut two thin strips of thick paper 3 in. long. Ask a grown-up to help you curl them along the edge of scissors. Glue on to closed end of peg.

4

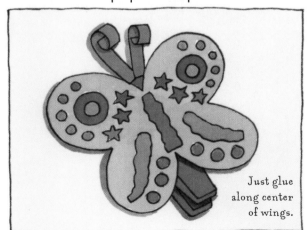

Just glue along center of wings.

Glue butterfly wings on pin below antennae. Clip onto the edges of lampshades or use it to keep your boots together.

Modeling marzipan

Fruits

These pretty fruits can be used to decorate cakes or be given as presents in small baskets (see pages 18 and 19) or boxes. Make delicious home-made marzipan or you can use bought marzipan—white is best if you want to color it.

★ 3.5 oz. (100 g) ground almonds
★ 3.5 oz. (100 g) mixed caster and icing sugar
★ 2 tsp lemon juice
★ egg white
★ bowl
★ spoon
★ plastic bag

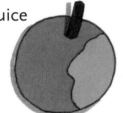

Roll marzipan strawberries in caster sugar.

Mold into fruit shapes and paint with food coloring.

Use cloves for stalks, eyes, and nose (but don't eat them).

1 Mix the ground almonds, sugars, and lemon juice in the bowl.

2 Add a very small amount of egg white and mix throughly until the paste is very stiff.

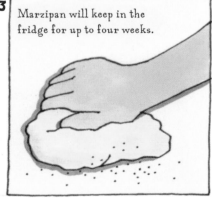

3 Marzipan will keep in the fridge for up to four weeks.

Knead paste on a surface dusted with icing sugar. Keep in a plastic bag until you want to use it.

chick

what you will need

★ homemade or bought white marzipan
★ yellow and red food coloring and paintbrush
★ 2 cloves

Roll the marzipan into two balls—one larger than the other. Keep a tiny bit aside.

Push the smaller ball on top of the other. Form the leftover piece into a beak and put it in place.

Paint the chick yellow. When dry paint the beak red and push cloves in for eyes.

Rabbit

★ homemade or bought white marzipan
★ blue food coloring and paintbrush
★ 3 cloves

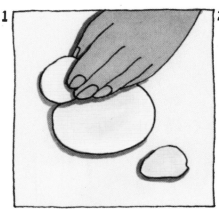

Roll the marzipan into two balls—one larger than the other. Keep a tiny bit aside.

Push the smaller ball on top of the other. Form the leftover piece into a tail and two ears.

Paint the rabbit blue leaving the tail white. Push cloves in for eyes and nose.

Frog bean bag

Make one frog to sit on a shelf or three to juggle with. Vary the patterns and colors of the fabric.

Before you begin
Ask a grown-up to help you iron out creases in the fabric.

What you will need
★ tracing paper and pencil
★ patterned fabric
★ scissors and pins
★ needle and thread
★ paintbrush
★ dried beans
★ small piece of felt
★ glue (if you want)

1

Ask a grown-up to help you cut it out carefully.

Trace frog template (on opposite page) onto tracing paper and pin onto two layers of fabric.

2

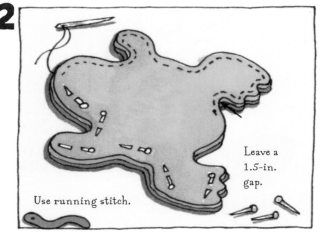

Leave a 1.5-in. gap.

Use running stitch.

Remove tracing paper and pin fabric together with patterned sides facing inwards. Sew 0.5 in. in from edge.

3

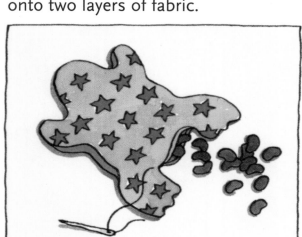

Turn inside out, pushing into corners with the end of the paintbrush. Fill with beans until full but still floppy.

4

Sew up gap very firmly. Cut out small felt circles for the eyes and glue or sew them on.

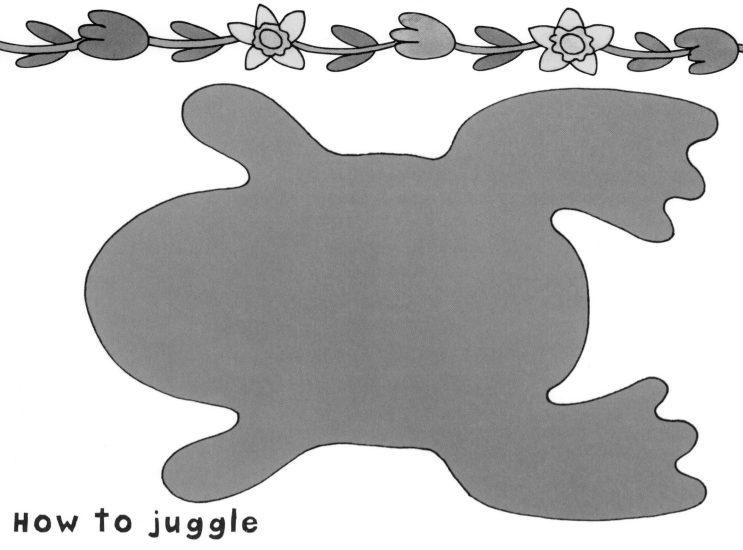

How to juggle

Juggling takes practice but it's great fun. Stand relaxed with your elbows near your body and your hands at waist height. Hold balls or frog bags in the palm of your hands. Use a scooping movement as you throw.

Try throwing two balls to and fro to begin with, throwing up in an arc. Don't throw the second ball until the first has started to come down. Now try with three balls or bags.

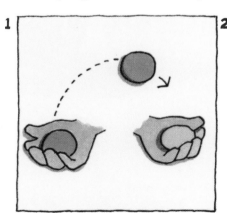

1 Throw one of the bags (from the two bag hand) up into an arc over to the (one bag) hand.

2 As the first bag begins to fall throw the bag held in the receiving hand in an arc, to the other hand.

3 As this bag starts to fall throw the third bag up and so on.

29

Easter weather

Spring, and therefore Easter in the Nothern Hemisphere, is a time of varied weather. Because Easter can be as much as a month apart from one year to the next there might be snow one year and sunshine the next.

Long before modern weather forecasts, people looked at the sky, trees, and the way birds and animals behaved to see what the weather would be like.

See if these old sayings are true.

Red sky at night, shepherd's delight,
Red sky in the morning, shepherd's warning.

Rain in the night,
Next day will be bright.

Rain before seven,
Fine before eleven.

If the rooks build high
the weather will be dry.

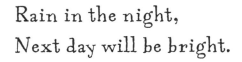

When the stars begin to muddle,
The earth will soon become a puddle.

Easter, Recycled!

In this section you will find lots more lovely projects for Easter decorations, gifts, and recipes. These projects use materials that you might have thrown away. Your pocket money will not only go a long way but you will also help the planet.

Have a look at pages 4 and 5 to see all the kinds of things you can keep to recycle. Old clothes, plastic bags, and cardboard boxes are not rubbish at all! The symbol ♺ in the list of things for each project shows you where you can use them. There are also template shapes and simple instructions on how to use them on page 50.

Use good glue (but not superglue).

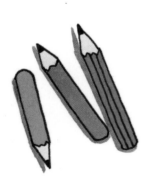

Make sure your pencils are sharp.

Use sharp, clean scissors

Before you start on a project make sure you read it through and get everything you need ready. Work on a clean, flat surface with plenty of room. If you need to use scissors, knives, the iron, or the oven be careful and have an adult standing by.

Easter gifts

cushion cover

You can use any size of old shirt to make this handy present. Just make sure that it fits the size of cushion pad you have.

✿ old clean shirt ♻
✿ ruler
✿ marker pen
✿ pins
✿ needle and thread
✿ scissors
✿ cushion pad

Use the marker pen.

Iron the shirt and do up the buttons. Lie it flat on a table. Keep the buttons centered and mark out a square, using your cushion pad as a guide. Pin both sides of the shirt together.

Cut the square out, leaving 0.5 in. extra around the pins. Remove the pins. Put right sides of fabric together. Pin again.

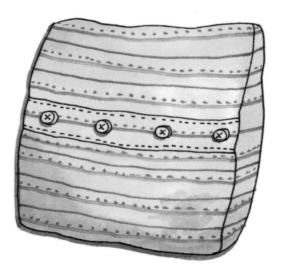

Sew around all four sides using running stitch.

Undo the buttons and turn right side out. Put in the cushion pad and button up.

Button Bracelet

You can use different sizes and colors of old buttons for these great bracelets. About twenty buttons should do. You can use two- or four-hole buttons.

- ❀ buttons
- ❀ 23.5 in. thin, round elastic
- ❀ darning needle
- ❀ sticky tape
- ❀ scissors

Continue adding more buttons in the same way. Push each one down to the last. You will find that they alternate the way they face.

Thread the needle with the elastic and knot the end. Pass it through the first button and secure with sticky tape.

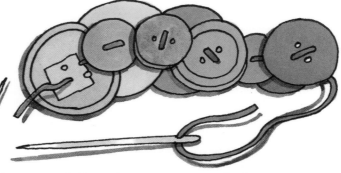

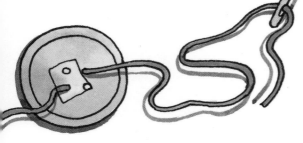

Keep adding buttons until the bracelet will fit around your wrist. Make it longer if it is for an adult. Remember it will stretch!

Pass the needle through two holes of the next button and push it down to the first.

Remove the sticky tape. Take the needle off the elastic. Tie ends firmly together and trim.

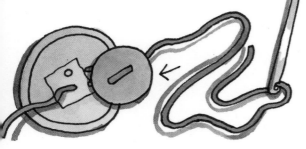

Bunch of Flowers

This unusual bouquet would make a lovely present, and lasts a lot longer than real flowers!

For 6 flowers

* ✿ cardboard egg carton ♻
* ✿ green drinking straws (bendy if possible)
* ✿ paints and brush
* ✿ sticky tape
* ✿ old giftwrap ♻
* ✿ scissors

Cut each cup into a flower. Cut four petals following the shape of the cup.

Cut the top off the egg-box. Then cut between the six egg sections so that you have six little cups. They don't look anything like flowers yet but don't worry!

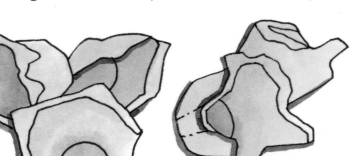

Paint the center of the flowers yellow or white. Paint the rest of the flowers in bright colors. Leave to dry.

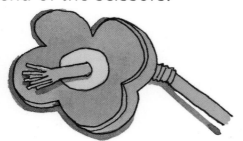

Make a small hole in the center of the flower with the end of the scissors.

Push the end of a straw, near the bendy part, into the hole. (It should be a tight fit.) Cut the end of the straw into a fringe. Pull gently so that the fringed end is near the hole.

Wrapping the Bouquet

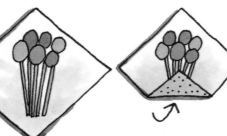

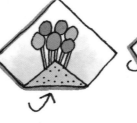

Place the flowers on the giftwrap.

Turn up the bottom.

Fold both sides in and secure with tape.

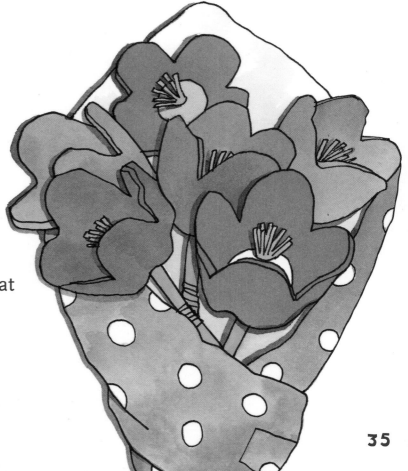

Easter cards

Floral Shapes

🌸 old magazines and catalogues ↻
🌸 colored paper, 8 in. x 6 in. ↻
🌸 pencil and tracing paper
🌸 glue and scissors

Fold the colored paper in half.

Look through old magazines and catalogues for pictures of flowers.

Use the templates and instructions on page 52 to trace and cut out floral shapes.

Glue onto the front of the card. Write a message inside.

Seed Packet

A card with a gift inside!

* colored paper, 8 in. x 6 in. ↻
* packet of flower seeds
* old magazine ↻
* sticky tape or stapler
* scissors
* glue
* pencil and tracing paper

Fold the colored paper in half. Trace one of the flower templates from page 52 on to the front of the card. Open out and cut the shape out of the card.

Tape or staple the packet of seeds inside the card opposite the cut-out.

Close the card. Cut out shapes of a stem and some leaves from the magazine.

Write a message inside the card.

Vintage Lace cards

Cut up lace doilies, mats, and any oddments to create an unusual and pretty lace picture.

* plain scrap paper
* pencil
* stiff, colored paper, 8 in. x 6 in.
* scraps of lace ⟳
* scissors
* glue

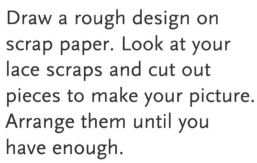

Draw a rough design on scrap paper. Look at your lace scraps and cut out pieces to make your picture. Arrange them until you have enough.

38

Fold the colored paper in half. Start gluing down the lace bits on the front of it to form your picture. Cut thin strips for stalks and leaves. Glue flowers on the top.

Make a vase out of different pieces.

Overlap some of the lace but not all of it. Then the lace will show up well against the colored paper.

Use strips of lace to make grasses and reeds.

Small pieces of net form water ripples.

Festive Food

Stuffed Hard-boiled Eggs

You can make as many of these as you need.

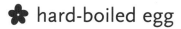

* hard-boiled egg
* 1 heaped teaspoon mayonnaise
* curry powder to taste
* salt and pepper
* lettuce leaves to serve

Peel the egg when it is cool.
Cut it in half lengthways.
Scoop out the yolk from
each half and place in a bowl.

Carefully spoon the yolk
mixture back into the egg
halves. Place on top of
lettuce leaves to serve.

Add the mayonnaise, curry powder,
salt, and pepper. Mix it well.

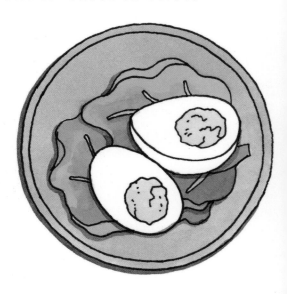

Quick Pea Soup

A very easy recipe with a pretty green color and a fresh minty taste.

Serves 2

- ❀ 7 oz. (200 g) frozen peas
- ❀ 20 fl. oz. (600 ml) chicken or vegetable stock
- ❀ 1 heaped tablespoon chopped fresh mint
- ❀ 2 tablespoons Greek yogurt or fromage frais
- ❀ salt and pepper to taste

Place everything in a blender and whiz until smoothish. There will be a few bits of pea and mint left. If you prefer it smooth simply pour the soup through a sieve before serving.

Put the peas and stock into a saucepan and simmer for 3–4 minutes until the peas are cooked.

Lemon cupcakes

These delicious little cakes are perfect for passover.

Makes 12

- ✿ 4.5 oz. (125 g) self-raising flour
- ✿ 4.5 oz. (125 g) very soft, unsalted butter
- ✿ 4.5 oz. (125 g) caster sugar
- ✿ 2 eggs
- ✿ grated zest of 1 lemon
- ✿ 1 teaspoon lemon juice
- ✿ 1 tablespoon milk

Add the milk and whiz again until the mixture is smooth and drops easily off a spoon.

Preheat the oven to 200°C/400°F.

Simply place all the ingredients except the milk into a food processor and whiz them together.

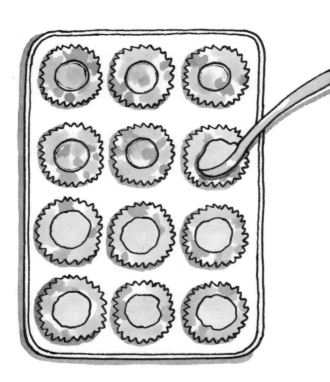

Place 12 paper cases in a bun or muffin tin. Spoon the mixture evenly into the cases.

Bake for about 20 minutes in the center of the oven. The cakes should be golden and springy to the touch. Cool on a wire rack.

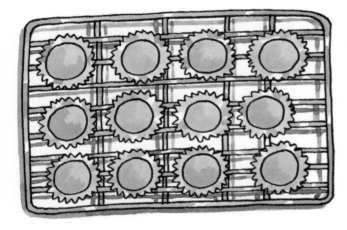

Lemon Icing

❀ 7 oz. (200 g) sifted icing sugar
❀ juice of half a lemon
❀ yellow food coloring
❀ yellow, green, or white cake decorations

Mix the sugar and lemon juice in a bowl until smooth. Use a knife dipped in hot water to spread the icing on top of six of the cakes.

Then add a few drops of coloring to the icing before icing the rest.

Add decorations to finish.

Easter Decorations

Shiny chains

These look great hanging up in windows to catch the light.

* plastic bottles, all sizes and colors
* old magazine
* sticky tape and glue
* scissors

Throw the bottle caps away.
Wash the bottles and remove bottle labels. Cut the neck of the bottle off. It is quite hard to cut into the bottles to start with so ask an adult to help.

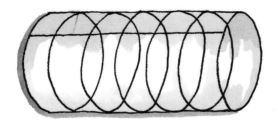

Cut the bottle lengthways down to the end. Then cut it into rings about 1 in. wide.

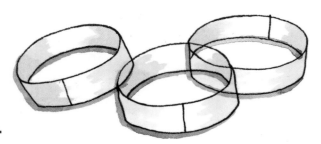

Cut small flowers or spots of color from the magazine. Glue these around the rings.

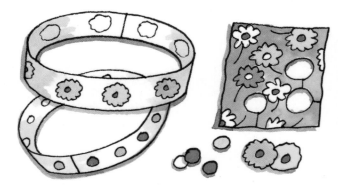

Join the rings together into chains by opening them and securing with small pieces of sticky tape.

Hang them up.

Fancy Eggs

Make one for each of your guests. Place them in a bowl on the table or at each place setting.

* eggs
* darning needle
* thin, colored paper or foil
* small, sharp scissors
* glue
* pencil and tracing paper
* pinking shears

To empty each egg: Wash the egg. Use the needle to make a small hole at the narrow end of the egg and a larger hole at the other end.

Hold the egg over a bowl and blow through the smaller hole.

Cut a narrow strip of paper long enough to fit around the egg lengthways. Cut two more strips with pinking shears in another color. Glue them around the egg. Leave to dry.

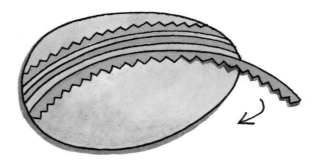

Templates

Choose one of the templates. Copy it twice onto the paper. Cut them out and glue one on each side of the egg. Rub them on carefully.

See the instructions on page 55 for how to use these templates.

Daisies

These are such fun and so quick to make that you won't want to stop! Use them to decorate bags, hats, hairbands, or make a brooch.

They can be made out of yarn, string, thin ribbon, or raffia. To make smaller or larger daisies simply alter the size of the cardboard circle.

❁ thick cardboard ↻
❁ pencil and compass
❁ scissors
❁ 12 pins with round heads
❁ darning needle
❁ yarn ↻

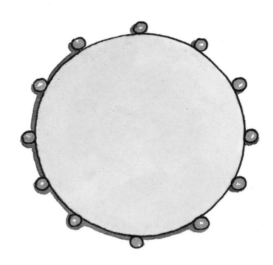

Draw and cut out a card circle 2 in. in diameter. Push the pins into the card edge at regular spaces like a clock face.

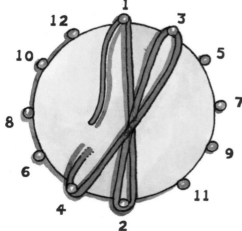

Hold the end of the yarn with your left thumb on the card circle. Pass the yarn around pin 1 left to right and then back across the circle to pin 2 opposite. At pin 2 pass the yarn right to left and then across to pin 3 left to right.

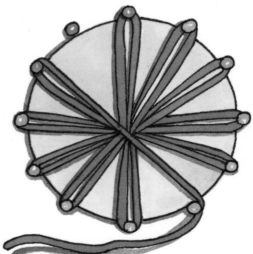

Carry on winding the yarn around the pins in the same way, working in a clockwise direction. Wrap more than once around if you are using thin yarn, but just once if you yarn is thick.

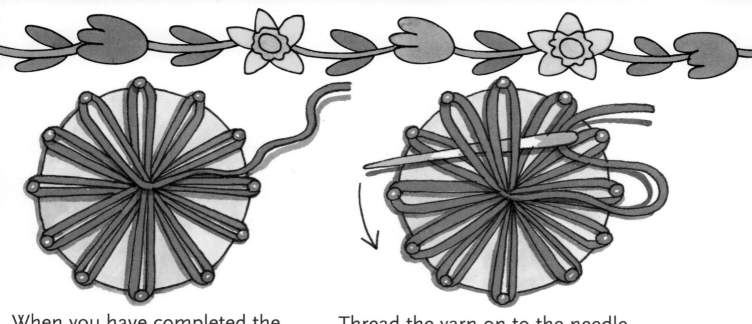

When you have completed the daisy petals cut off the yarn, leaving an extra 12-in. length.

Thread the yarn on to the needle. Pass the yarn under two petals and back over one. Continue in this way until all twelve petals are secured. Pass the end of the yarn through the center to finish. Knot and cut off.

Pull out the pins and turn the daisy over.

Use a different colored yarn to sew a center.

Sew buttons or beads into the center.

Easter Bonnets

Dawn Chorus

✿ 2 strips stiff, colored paper, about 24 in. x 2 in. ↻

✿ twigs ↻

✿ small pieces of colored paper ↻

✿ felt-tip pen

✿ pencil and tracing paper

✿ sticky tape and glue

✿ scissors

Tape the strip together to fit around your head and put it on!

Attach the twigs to one of the paper strips with sticky tape.

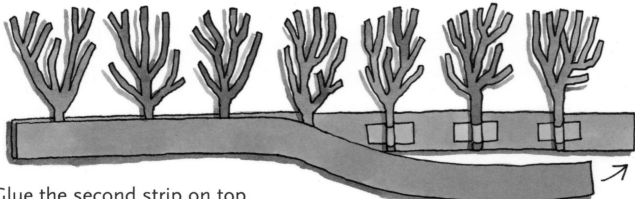

Glue the second strip on top.
Use the little bird template and instructions on pages 52 and 55 to trace and cut out lots of birds in different colors. Glue them on to the twigs.

Add eyes and wing detail in felt-tip.

Spring crown

- strip of stiff, colored paper, about 24 in. x 2 in.
- stiff, colored paper
- buttons
- pencil and tracing paper
- glue and scissors
- felt-tip pens

Use the rabbit and flower templates and instructions on pages 52 and 55 to trace and cut out four rabbits and four flowers in different colors.

Stick them along the paper strip.

Glue on buttons and add details with felt-tip pens.

Pull the strip around in a crown and glue the ends together to fit your head.

Ducks on a Pond

- thick cardboard (from a box)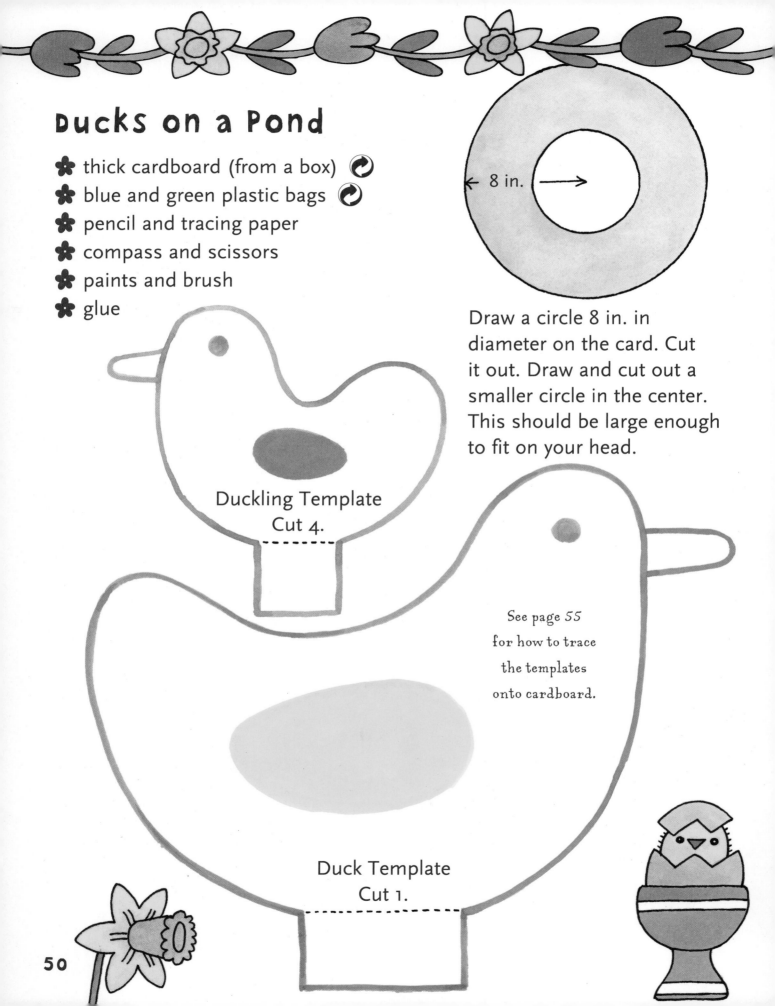
- blue and green plastic bags
- pencil and tracing paper
- compass and scissors
- paints and brush
- glue

← 8 in. →

Draw a circle 8 in. in diameter on the card. Cut it out. Draw and cut out a smaller circle in the center. This should be large enough to fit on your head.

Duckling Template
Cut 4.

See page 55 for how to trace the templates onto cardboard.

Duck Template
Cut 1.

Paint both sides of the duck and ducklings. Leave to dry.

Score the tabs on the bottom of the ducks and bend. Glue the tabs on to the card ring to position the ducks in a ring.

Cut the plastic bags into strips. Glue on to the ring so that they cover the tabs. Overlap the plastic and glue underneath the ring too. Keep the plastic ruffled so that it looks like water.

51

Template Shapes

1. Trace a shape on to tracing paper.

2. Turn over and scribble over lines.

3. Turn over again and retrace over lines on to paper, card or fabric.

Floral Shapes Card

Dawn Chorus

Floral Shapes Card and Spring Crown

Seed Packet Card and Spring Crown

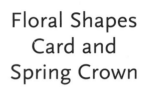

Floral Shapes Card

Seed Packet Card

MAKE AND COLOR

Paper

Decorations

How to make these Easter paper decorations

On pages 65 to 84 there are ready-drawn cards, decorations, and Easter things for you to color. Color the ready-drawn shapes first. Use colored pencils, crayons, felt-tip pens, or paints. Color from the center to the edges to avoid smudging. Use fairly thick paint and wash your brush between colors. Leave the cut-outs flat to dry, then cut them out along the solid lines, and fold along dotted lines.

On page 63 there is a template which can be used to make envelopes for your cards.

There are lots of ideas on how to make more Easter things. There are also templates and stencils to help you.

Some things you will need:
- ❖ plain and colored paper or thin cardboard
- ❖ tracing paper
- ❖ pencil, ruler
- ❖ scissors, craft knife
- ❖ sticky tape, glue
- ❖ string or yarn
- ❖ crayons, paints, and felt-tip pens
- ❖ foils from chocolate eggs and candies
- ❖ colored tissue papers

Be careful when using a craft knife.

Templates

Here is how to trace simply and successfully from the templates.

What you will need
★ tracing paper
★ soft pencil
★ sticky tape
★ paper or card

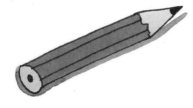

1

Tape a piece of tracing paper over the template. Trace a shape with the pencil.

2

Turn over the tracing paper and scribble over the lines with the pencil.

3

Turn over again and tape on to some cardboard or paper. Retrace firmly over the lines. Remove the tracing paper.

Stencils

Cut or pull out the sheet of stencils from the back of the book. Follow the instructions below on how to use them.

what you will need:
❖ colored paper or card
❖ pencil, crayons, and felt tips
❖ scissors

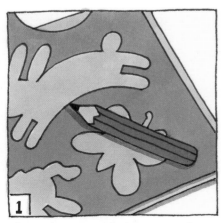

1

Place the stencil shape on the cardboard or paper. Draw inside the shape with a pencil.

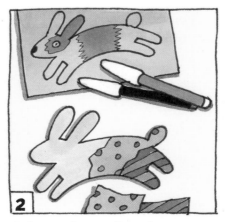

2

Color in the outline shape or cut it out with scissors. Use it to make Easter things.

Table decorations

Make a chicken or rabbit as a jolly decoration for an Easter celebration.

Easter chicken

Paint a paper plate for the chicken body and leave it to dry. Then trace the head and tail templates below (see page 55).
Cut out two of each, one for each side.

Glue the tops of the head and tail pieces together where shown by the grey area on the template. Paint both sides.

Fold the paper plate in half and paint a wing on each side of the plate.

Push the head and tail over the folded edge of the plate and glue them in place.

what you will need:

❖ stiff paper or thin cardboard
❖ large paper plate
❖ scissors
❖ tracing paper, pencil
❖ felt tip pens, paints
❖ glue
❖ large plate
❖ tissue paper
❖ small sugar or chocolate eggs

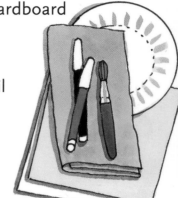

Cut green tissue into fringes to make grass. Arrange it on the plate and hide little eggs in it.

chicken head template

Glue area
(marked in grey)

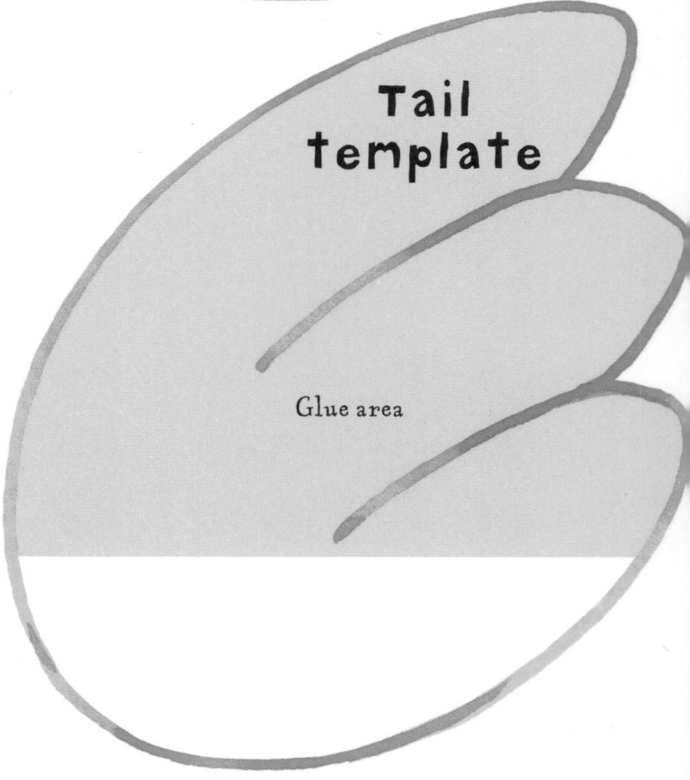

Tail template

Glue area

Easter rabbit

Paint a paper plate in bright colors then leave it to dry. Trace the rabbit template on this page, and cut out two. Glue the tops of the shapes together where shown by the grey area on the template. Decorate both sides.

Fold the plate in half and push the double rabbit over the folded edge. Glue it in place.

Open out the two sides.

Push the rabbit on to the plate.

Glue area

Rabbit template

Foil fun

Collect the colored foil from candies and Easter eggs. Unwrap them carefully. Smooth out the foil with your finger or the back of a spoon and keep it flat.

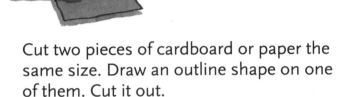

Easter cards

Draw an outline using the stencils from pages 83 and 84. See the instructions on page 55. Glue different foils inside the shape.

Cut two pieces of cardboard or paper the same size. Draw an outline shape on one of them. Cut it out.

Glue colored foils onto the other sheet and then glue the two pieces together so that the foils pattern shows through the cut-out shape.

Easter garlands

Draw and cut out several of the Easter egg and bow stencil shapes on pages 83 and 84. Decorate them with colored foils, and then string them up to make an Easter garland.

HAPPY EASTER

Screw up bits of foil into sausage shapes or balls and use them to decorate your Easter shapes.

Easter time!

Make this Easter clock and turn the hands to mark the time of your Easter celebrations.

Trace the clock and hands below on to thin card (see the template instructions on page 55). Decorate them, then cut them out.

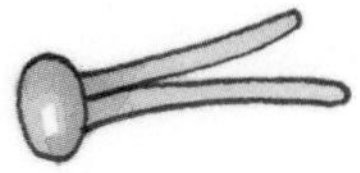

Attach the hands through the center of the clock with a paper fastener, where marked.

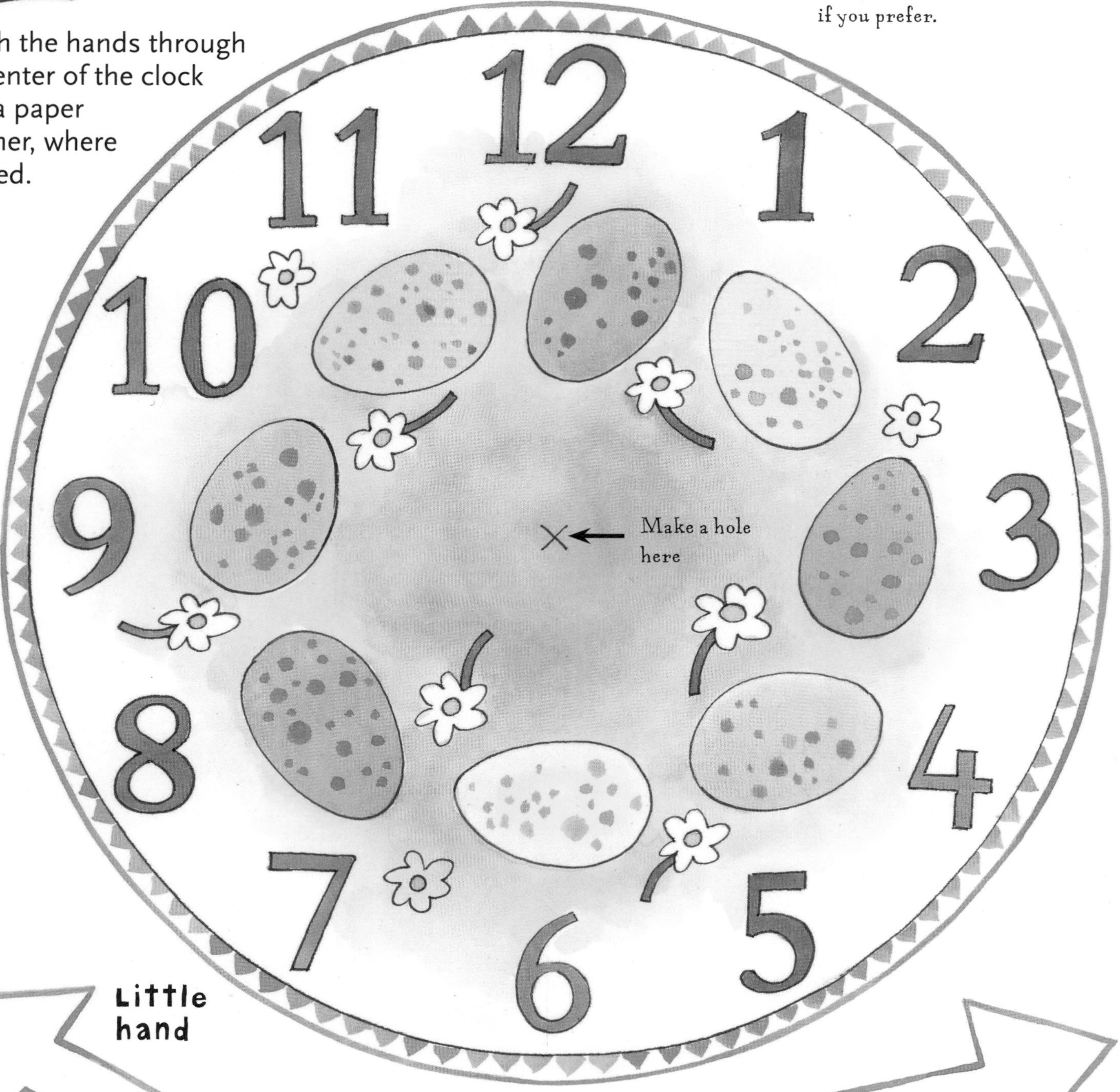

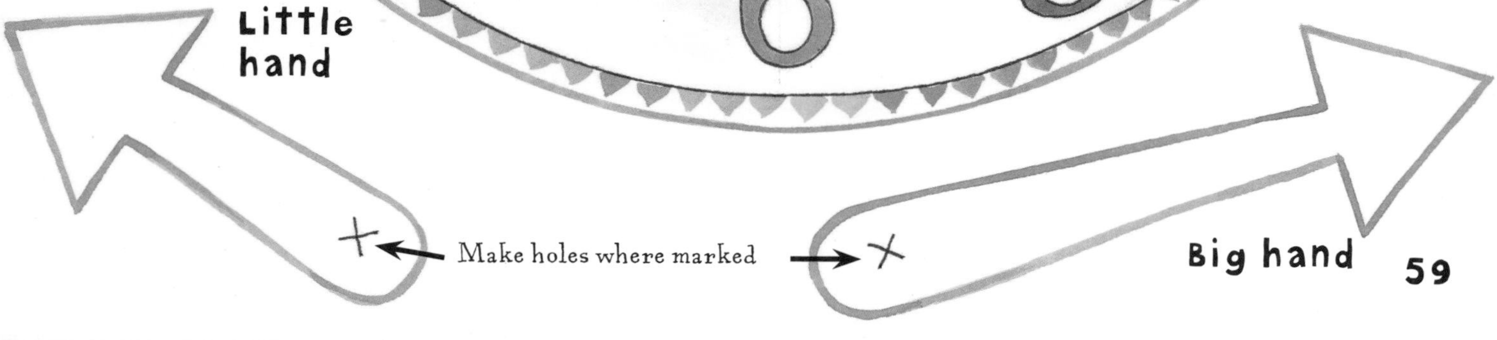

Design your own decoration, if you prefer.

× ← Make a hole here

Little hand

Big hand

× ← Make holes where marked → ×

Envelopes

Make some colorful envelopes using the template on page 63. Send your family and friends the Easter cards you have made!

What you will need:
★ colored paper
★ pencil
★ tracing paper
★ ruler
★ scissors
★ glue

1

Follow the instructions on page 55 to trace the template on to paper, using a ruler to help. Cut it out.

2

Fold along the dotted lines. Glue the bottom flap on to the two side flaps. Put in your card and glue down the top flap.

Decorate your envelopes using the templates on pages 2 and 3.

Nan

Mrs. M Rabbit
The Warren,
Easter Hill.

Templates

Follow the instructions on page 55
to use the templates on the following pages

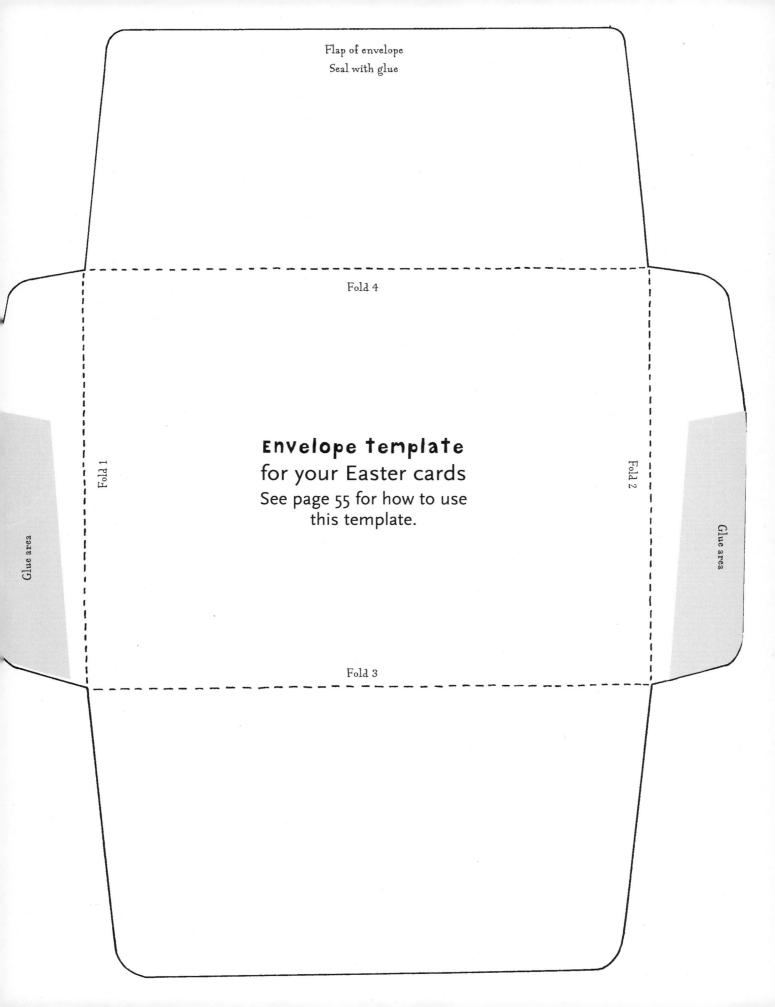

Flap of envelope
Seal with glue

Fold 4

Glue area

Fold 1

Envelope template
for your Easter cards
See page 55 for how to use
this template.

Fold 2

Glue area

Fold 3

Flap of envelope
Seal with glue

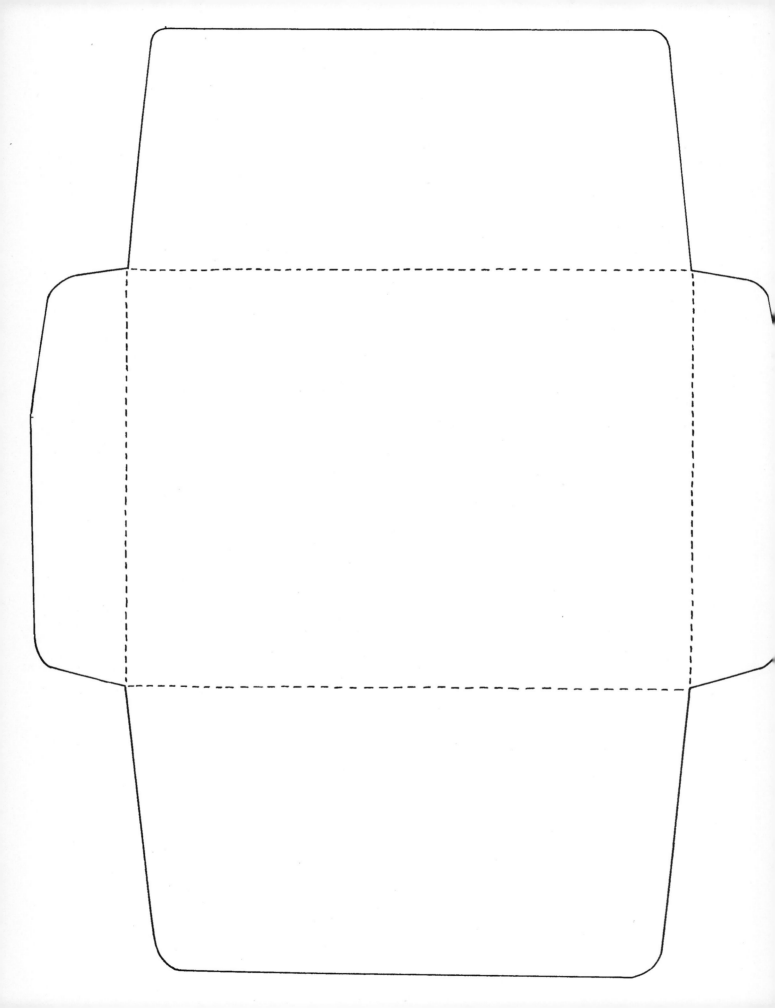

Gift tag templates

Trace these templates onto cardboard using the instructions on page 55, and color them in. Push a pencil through the black dot to make a hole, then make a tie with colored yarn.

Jug of flowers

Color in the flowers and the jug, then cut them out. Write an Easter
message inside the oval shape on the jug. Cut along the slot
marked at the top of the jug and push the flowers through the slot,
as shown below. Fix them in place with sticky tape on the back.
You can stand this colorful jug up
on a windowsill, shelf, or mantelpiece.

Be careful when
using the craft knife.

front

back

Cut out
handle

Easter basket

Decorate the basket, then it cut out along solid lines. Fold in the sides and the flaps along the dotted lines, then glue the basket together. Finally, glue the ends of the handle inside the basket.

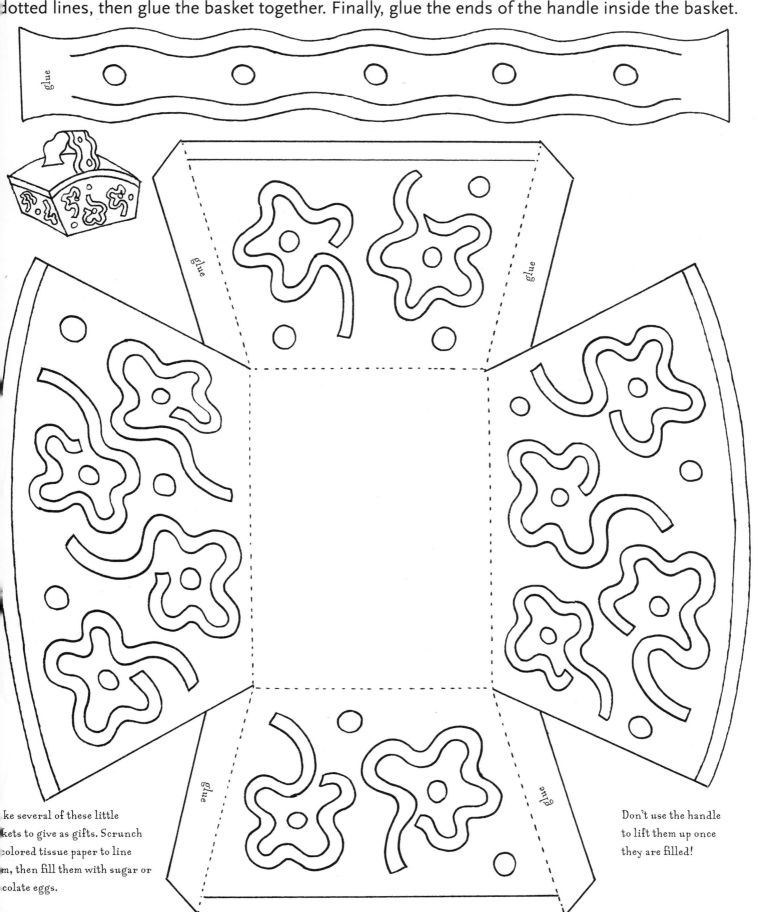

...ke several of these little
...kets to give as gifts. Scrunch
...colored tissue paper to line
...m, then fill them with sugar or
...colate eggs.

Don't use the handle
to lift them up once
they are filled!

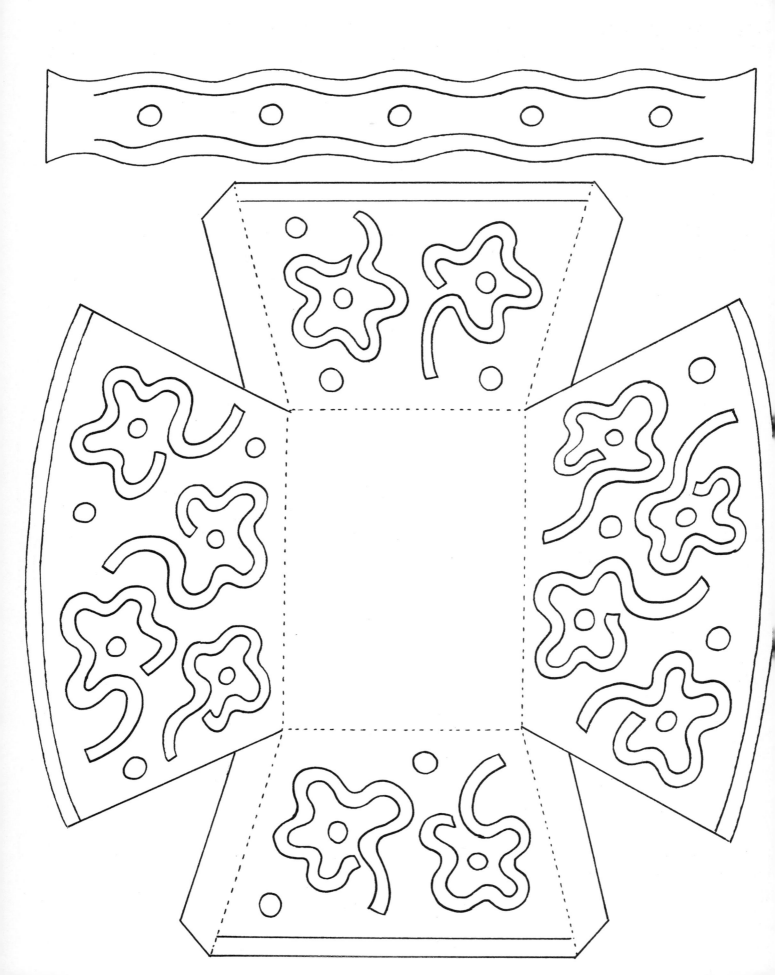

Place names

Color in the chicks and eggs, rabbits and hats, then cut them out. With a craft knife, carefully cut the slits on the eggs and hats, and around the rabbit arms and chick wings, as shown. Push the chicks and rabbits through the slots.

Push through slot

Bob

Kate

Write names on the cards and put one next to each person's place at the table.

Cut out the chick wings, rabbit arms, and the slits where marked by a thicker line.

Trace these shapes to make more, if you need them.

Bunny wishes you
a happy Easter

HAVE A
CRACKING
EASTER!

Color in, fold along dotted line, then cut out the shape around the outline, through both thicknesses. Write message in oval.

Cut out here

Cut around outline

FOLD

HAVE A
BOUNCY
EASTER

pring pencil tops

olor in the shapes then cut them out.
old each one in half down the center and
arefully cut out the holes marked in grey.
ush them onto pencil ends as Easter
ecorations or gifts.

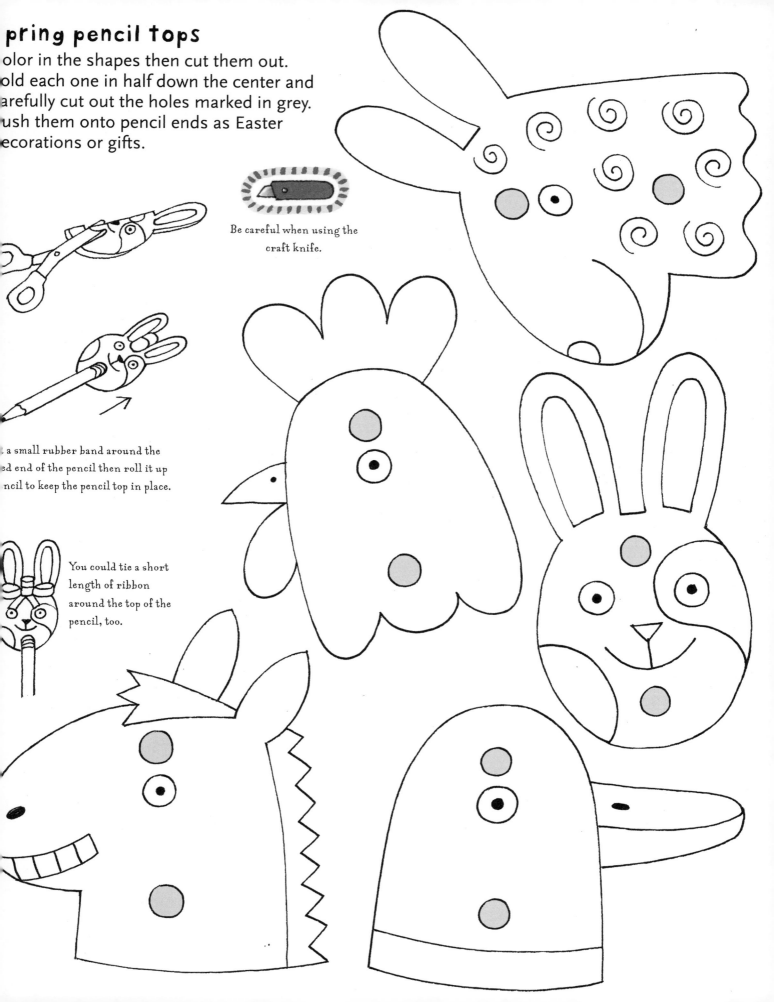

Be careful when using the
craft knife.

a small rubber band around the
ed end of the pencil then roll it up
ncil to keep the pencil top in place.

You could tie a short
length of ribbon
around the top of the
pencil, too.

easure hunt

en you have made some Easter baskets, why not have a
asure hunt to find them? Color in these eggs and cut them out,
en write clues on the back. A friend or relative could follow the
il of clues to find their Easter surprise.

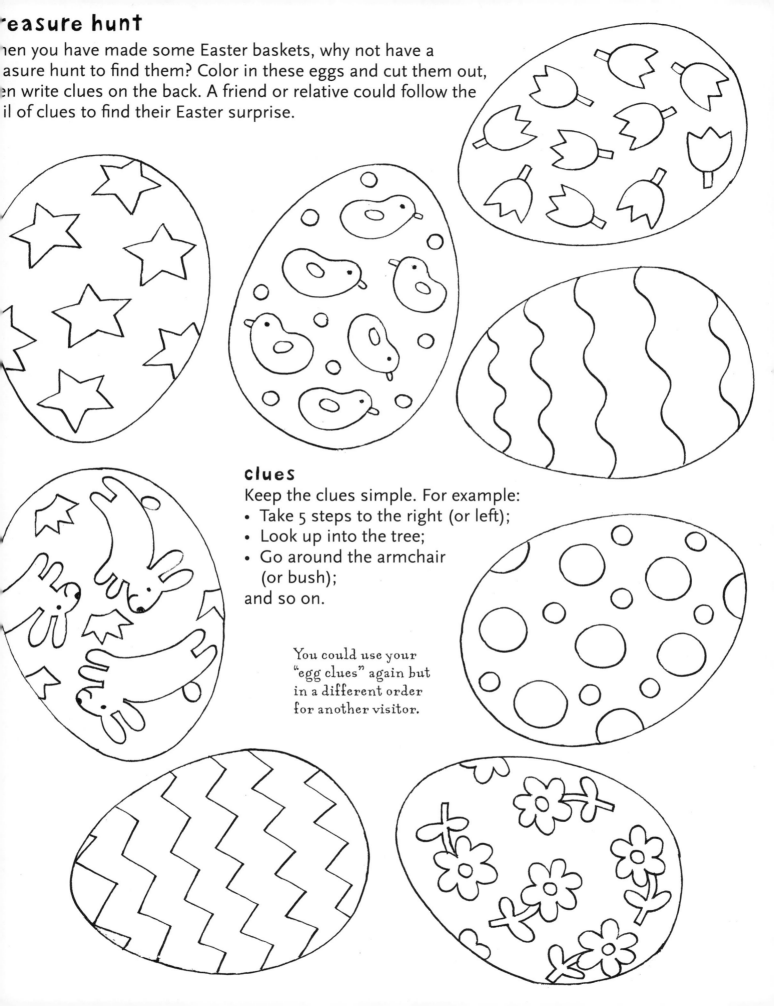

clues

Keep the clues simple. For example:

- Take 5 steps to the right (or left);
- Look up into the tree;
- Go around the armchair
  (or bush);

and so on.

You could use your
"egg clues" again but
in a different order
for another visitor.

MAKE AND COLOR
Easter on the Farm

country landscapes

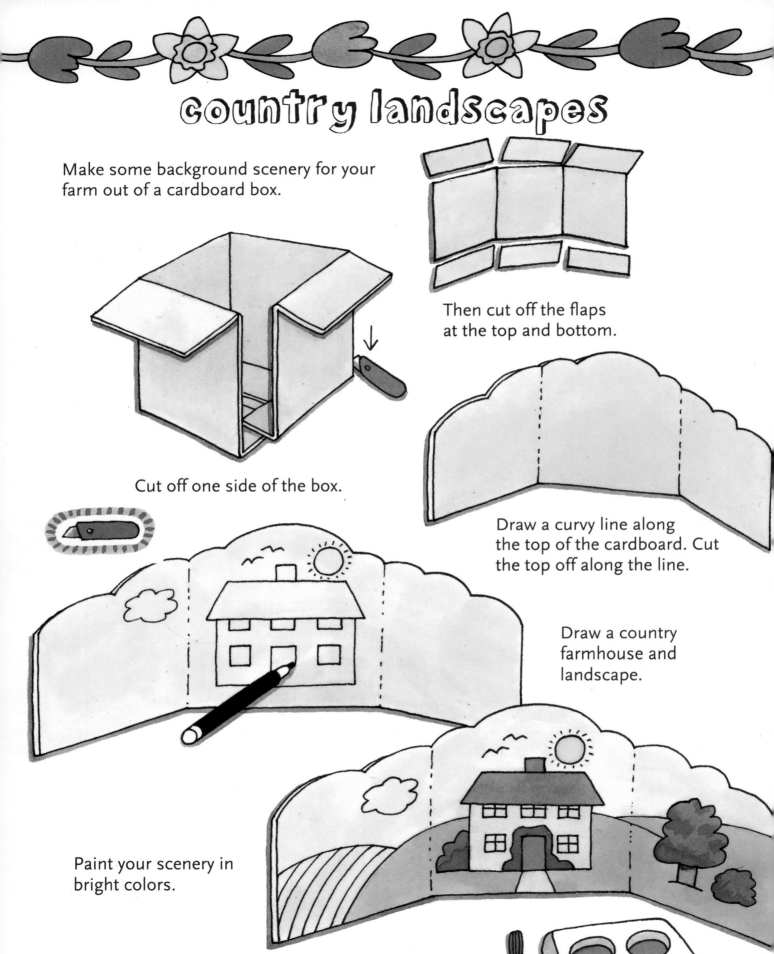

Make some background scenery for your farm out of a cardboard box.

Then cut off the flaps at the top and bottom.

Cut off one side of the box.

Draw a curvy line along the top of the cardboard. Cut the top off along the line.

Draw a country farmhouse and landscape.

Paint your scenery in bright colors.

Farm animals and figures

Color in the shapes then cut them out, then color the other side. Cut the slots at the TOP of the legs and push onto the animals.

Slot the wings on to the hens, ducks, etc., straight side up. Then bend them back a little.

When you have slotted the pieces together, you could use sticky tape to fix them more securely, if you like.

Rooster wings

calf

calf legs

Piglets

Horse

Horse legs

Donkey

Lamb

Lamb legs

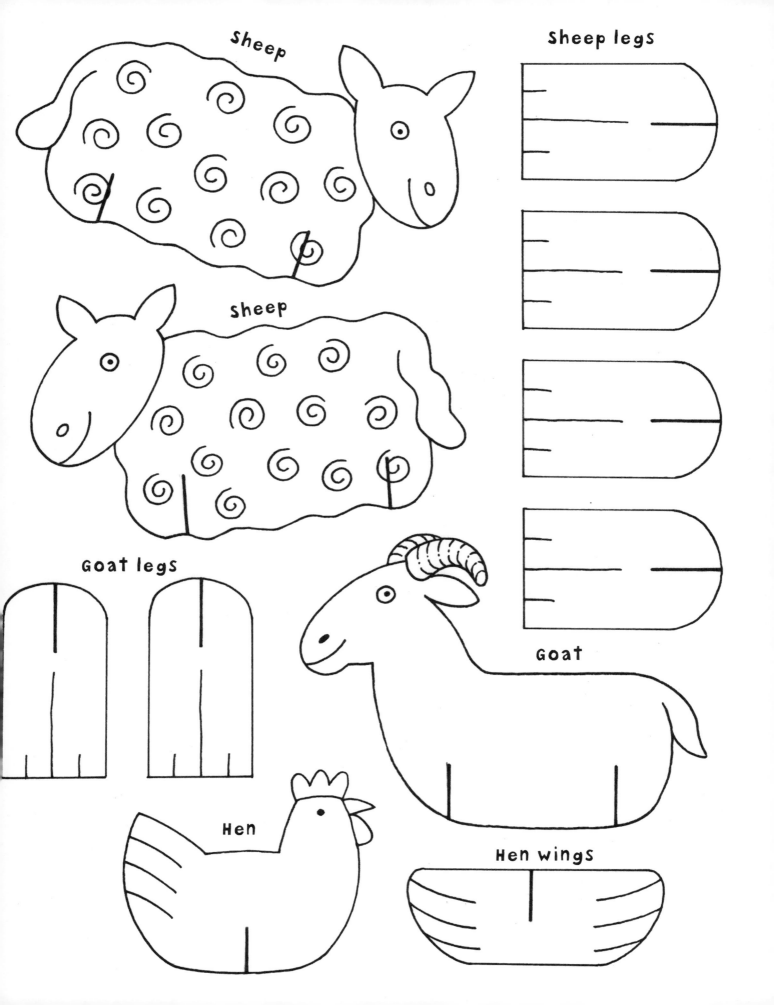

Sheep

Sheep legs

Sheep

Goat legs

Goat

Hen

Hen wings

cow legs

cow

cow

cow leg

Hen wings

Hen

Answers

See the 10 differences below to the spot the difference on page 24.